Enjoy the circus!

Mary Jo. Nyssen

ISBN: 0998583200

ISBN: 13:9780998583204

Library of Congress Control Number   2017900222

MOM-BA-BOOKS

Salem, OR

I dedicate this book to all my family who have been so supportive of my writing, and especially to my granddaughter, Hannah, grandson, Luke, and in memory of my grandson, Jacob, who passed away December 3, 2014.

Introduction to the reader of
"An Amazing Circus of Phonograms-Act 2"

In my first book, *A Colorful Journey Through the Land of Talking Letters,* and my second book, *An Amazing Circus of Phonograms – Act One,* I introduced the first 26 letters of the alphabet and the first 22 multi letter phonograms and their sounds. My third book which is Act Two, presents the remaining 22 multi letter phonograms, completing the 70 phonograms of the English language which children need to know to read, write and spell 80 percent of the English language. The 22 phonograms included in Act Two are **ng, ar, ck, ed, or, wh, ey, ei, ie, igh, eigh, kn, gn, wr, ph, dge, oe, gh, ti, si, ci** and **ough.**

Each phonogram which is being presented will be color high-lighted in the stories. **Those phonograms that have only one sound will be purple.** The phonograms that have more than one sound will be highlighted as follows: the first will be green, the second red, the third blue, the fourth orange, the fifth yellow and the sixth pink.

Some of the phonograms in Act Two, such as **gn, gh, ti, si, ci** and **ough,** present more difficult or unfamiliar words. Therefore, the parent or teacher, reading these stories, would need to explain the meaning of the words that the child is not familiar with. It also gives opportunity for children to learn to look these words up in the dictionary and expand their vocabulary. Knowing these 70 phonograms, presented in my three books, will help a child read, write and spell most words proficiently at an early age.

Come boys and girls and bring your treats!
Hurry along to take your seats!
Welcome back to the big top show!
The phonograms are ready to go
To share their sounds that you need to know!
Sit back and enjoy the fun,
For Act 2 has just begun!

"ng"
When **n** and **g** sing together, they make the sound as in long,
Rang, hung and song.

Introducing the amazing Ling,
Who is performing in the big top circus ring.
Ling sings as she swings through the air
On the flying trapeze without a care.
Bouncing and flipping on a trampoline,
Is her fearless and daunting brother, Bing.
What a stunning act done in the ring
By the daring Bing and dazzling Ling.

"ar"
Performing together, letters **a** and **r** say the name of the letter **r**
As in garden, car, far and star.

The variety show on the carpet is about to start.
Marvelous Martha and Martin each have their part.
Martha does cartwheels, wearing a leotard of scarlet lace,
While Martin juggles marshmallows standing in place.
What a spectacular performance for us today.
Thank you, Martha and Martin, for your remarkable display.

"ck"

Acting together, the letters **c** and **k** make the sound of **k** for you
When used after the short vowel sounds of **a,e,i,o** and **u**
As in sa**ck**, de**ck**, ki**ck**, blo**ck** and lu**ck**, to name a few.

In the center ring, Jack is performing his tricks.
From his magic black hat, he pulls out a clock that ticks,
A sparkling green necklace, a yellow rubber duck,
A silver nickel and a red toy truck.
Thank you for performing your hat trick act!
Next year, the circus wants you to come back.

"ed"

The letters **e** and **d** skate together to show you the past.
They have three sounds you are able to learn very fast.
Their first sound is like the man's name, "Ed,"
As in grad**ed**, seat**ed** and elect**ed**.

In the ice rink, provid**ed** in ring number two,
Hannah and her very talent**ed** cat, LuLu,
Came here to share the act they creat**ed** for you.
Hannah and Lulu, together, skat**ed** so nice.
Smoothly, they glid**ed** across the ice.
Wearing polka dott**ed** scarves, they twist**ed** in the air
And land**ed** quite gracefully without a care.
They present**ed** an A rat**ed** performance with plenty of flare.

"ed"
Their second sound is the same sound made by the letter **d**
In words such as answer**ed**, roll**ed**,
Cover**ed** and controll**ed**.

We welcom**ed** Bob and his bullfrog to the ring today,
Along with his dog, nam**ed** Buddy, who lov**ed** to play.
Buddy roll**ed** over and held up a hoop as high as he could,
While Bob's bullfrog leapfrogg**ed** through the hoop made of wood.
Bob cheer**ed** and yell**ed** for his pet bullfrog,
Amaz**ed** at the leap he did over Buddy, his dog.

"ed"
Their third sound makes the sound of the letter **t**
In words such as mixed, hoped and baked, as you can see.

Jacob promised to bring his brave and daring horse.
He laughed as he galloped around the course.
Then he jumped over the stacked bales of hay
And found a fresh baked pie in his way.
He chopped it in two for himself and his trusty steed.
Then they dashed from the ring to enjoy their pie feed.

"or"

Acting together, the letters **o** and **r** make their sound as in corn,
Storm, horn and born.

Morton is the most daring clown in our circus this morning.
His act is dangerous, and his orange motorcycle is roaring.
His collaborator, Jordan, lights the ring of fire with a torch.
Then Morton revs his motor and speeds around the course.
In his basket, he transports a bucket of corn seeds.
He honks his horn and gathers more speed.
His motorcycle zooms through the flaming circle of fire.
The corn pops like an enormous explosion, shooting higher and higher!
Morton's act is an extraordinary sight,
And the smell of popcorn is such a delight.

"wh"

When the letters **w** and **h** perform as one sound,
They make a breath sound, as we have found,
In words such as while and whimper,
Whip, wharf and whisper.

In the center ring is Admiral Wheeler, wearing his white naval uniform.
With him is his whimsical whale, Whitney, waiting to perform.
Wheeler whispers in her ear, and Whitney smiles with a whacky grin,
While whipping her tail and whistling a tune again and again.
What a whiz-bang act is this Whitney whale
With her whistling tune while whisking her tail.

"ey"
Joining together, the letters **e** and **y** have two sounds they say.
Their first sound says the long sound of the letter a
As in grey, obey, prey and survey.

Reynard joins us in the ring today
With his cat, Heyzell, and his handsome mouse, Mr. Grey.
Even though a cat's instinct is to chase a mouse as its prey,
Heyzell does a Spanish dance instead with the handsome Mr. Grey.
Hey now! This we surely can convey:
They are best pals, and Heyzell doesn't chase Mr. Grey as her prey.

"ey"
Their second sound says the long sound of the letter **e**
As in words like honey, monkey, turkey and key.

Now entering the ring is Ashley, dressed in a tutu made of money.
With Ashley are Courtney, her monkey, and Toney, her donkey.
Courtney plays the keyboard for a jar of honey.
Ashley balances gracefully on the back of Toney
As he prances around, nibbling a slab of baloney.
Ashley does a curtsey, while Courtney and Toney take a bow,
For their fantastic performance is over now.

"ei"
When the letters **e** and **i** get together to play,
They have two sounds they like to say.
The first sound is the long sound of **e** as in receive,
Leisure, weird and perceive.

Our next act is for all our circus guests.
Welcome Deidrich and Neil, who will put some tricks to the test.
On unicycles, they start circling leisurely around.
Neil juggles protein bars, and not one falls to the ground.
Deidrich balances on his head a protein shake with ease.
Let's hope that neither of these men will sneeze.
What an inconceivable thing that would be,
But they seize the day with a flawless act for all to see.

"ei"
Their second sound is the long sound of the letter **a**
In words such as beige, rein, veil and vein.

Princess Leilani rides into the circus ring today.
She wears a beige lacy veil and an orchid lei.
Leilani holds tightly onto the reins of her reindeer
And leads him to jump over bamboo sticks without fear.
Their act is stupendous, and so are they.
Thank you, Leilani, and your reindeer for being with us today.

"ie"

When the letters **i** and **e** work together, they make two sounds.
Their first sound is the long sound of the letter **e**
As in field, belief and achieve,
Yield, niece and relieve.

As the clowns come into the big top ring, we hear a shriek.
Chief Arnie is chasing Guthrie, the fierce thief of the week.
Guthrie took his niece, Annie, and stole all his gold;
And Arnie is retrieving what Guthrie mischievously stole.
Annie is relieved that Arnie achieved his goal.
Now Guthrie is in cuffs, to their relief;
And Arnie and Annie are free from their grief.

"ie"
Their second sound says the long sound of **i**
As in p**ie**, d**ie** and l**ie**.

Check out the clowns coming into ring two.
You will d**ie** of laughter with the things they do.
They sp**ie**d the fr**ie**d p**ie**s and tr**ie**d to twirl them on sticks.
As they rel**ie**d on their talent, they cr**ie**d, "Look at our tricks!"
They l**ie**d to us all, and down came the p**ie**s all over the place.
Collapsed on the ground, they sit with fr**ie**d p**ie** on their face.

"igh"

When the letters **i**, **g** and **h** act together,
They make the long sound of the letter **i**
As in flight, sigh, tight and high.

In the center ring is Dwight the White knight.
As he climbs the ladder, he is a mighty sight.
High on the tight wire, he stands bright and tall.
Dwight walks very slowly and not frightened at all.
He turns and very slightly jumps around,
Returning to the ladder with a mighty bound.
Dwight is a bright shining knight, so I've been told.
He walks on the tight wire and is courageous and bold.

"eigh"

When the letters **e**, **i**, **g** and **h** ride together, they say
The long sound of the letter **a**
In words such as **eigh**t, n**eigh**bor and w**eigh**.

Kay rides her sl**eigh** into the circus ring today.
Along with her is her n**eigh**bor, Ray.
They are used to loading heavy fr**eigh**t,
And Kay's horse, Faye, hauls tons of w**eigh**t.
Ray is lifting **eigh**ty pound w**eigh**ts, riding on Faye,
While Kay holds up an **eigh**t pound bale of fresh hay.
Faye n**eigh**s and continues to circle the ring with the sleigh.
Thank you, Kay, for bringing your n**eigh**bor, Ray, to the ring today.

"kn"
When Letters **k** and **n** are balancing together,
they say the sound of the letter **n** as in knack,
And can only be used at the beginning of a base word
as in knit and knapsack.

Knoll is wearing his knickers and knee-highs to our circus show.
While teetering on the knotty pine beam in the ring below,
On his head, he balances one of his favorite knick-knacks,
A courageous young knight, whom he named Sir Max,
Which Knoll had packed in his knitted knapsack.
Thank you, Knoll, for your balancing act
And sharing with us your favorite knick-knack.

"gn"

When the letters **g** and **n** ride together, they make the sound of **n** as in sign, gnu, gnat, gnome and design.

Into the ring comes the benign shaggy gnu, who is so good.
Mr. Gnome rides the gnu, standing on a gnarled piece of wood.
Out of his fantastic designer hat,
Mr. Gnome takes Nelly, the nice little gnat,
And places her on the gnu's straw hat.
Nelly performs a lively jig just like that.
What a cool act they brought to you.
Thank you, Mr. Gnome, Nelly gnat and gnu.

"wr"

When the letters **w** and **r** perform together,
The **w** is silent and allows **r** to say its sound
As in wrinkle, wring, wrong and wreath, we have found.

To the circus ring, welcome Wrisley and Wren, who are truly pros.
Wrisley balances a writing pen on his wrinkled nose,
While twirling wristwatches on his two big toes.
Wren wriggles a wreath like a plastic hoop around her hips,
While balancing a wrench on her finger tips.
What an astonishing act presented by Wrisley and Wren
With a wreath, a wrench, wristwatches and a writing pen.

"ph"
Playing together, the letters **p** and **h**
Make the sound of **f** as in prophet,
Elephant, paragraph, phone and alphabet.

In ring two, Philomena Elephant plays her saxophone.
Daphne Dolphin juggles letters of the alphabet all on her own.
Phillip Pheasant lights the canon and "Ka-boom!"
Phonograms shoot out all over the room.
What a triumphant performance for this threesome.
We are euphoric that they were able to come.

"dge"

As they trudge along, the letters **d**,**g** and **e** make the sound
of the letter **j** as in fudge,
And may only be used after a single vowel, saying its short vowel
sound in words such as badge, edge, bridge, lodge and budge.

We acknowledge Mrs. Partridge on stage with the circus judge,
Holding her huge wedge of blue ribbon chocolate fudge.
Mr. Hedgehog trudges behind with her badge for first place.
After seeing all the hodge podge of fudge in the race,
The judge chose Mrs. Partridge, and he would not budge,
Giving her first place for her superior fudge.

When the letters **o** and **e** act together, they want you to know,
They say the long sound of the letter **o** as in t**oe**.

A clown with big t**oe**s is here to put on a show.
In the center ring, we have M**oe** and J**oe**dy, his pet d**oe**.
J**oe**dy plays for us a w**oe**ful tune on her **oboe**,
While M**oe** stands on tipt**oe**, juggling rosy tomat**oe**s
And balancing on his head a basket of potat**oe**s.
M**oe** and his d**oe** really know how to put on a show
With tomat**oe**s and potat**oe**s and J**oe**dy's **oboe**.

"gh"

When **g** and **h** haunt together, the **h** doesn't make a sound for you,
And allows **g** to say its hard sound as in ghetto, aghast and ghoul.

Our ghoulish clowns have come back to haunt our circus today.
Ghoshel Ghost and Ghita, the ghostly girl, are here to play.
Ghoshel shoots spaghetti from his ghastly canon. It is a disaster!
Ghita, with a ghostly grin, juggles gherkins faster and faster.
After their act, Ghoshel and Ghita disappear just like that.
What a ghastly performance this was, to be exact.

"ti"
The letters **t** and **i** say, "**sh**," when they are together
in any syllable after the first one
As in nation, action, motion, creation and option.

Next, meet an addition to our international circus show,
The famous ambitious acrobats from Italy's region of Veneto.
Delfina does a collection of amazing somersaults. Watch her go!
Luke and Enzo patiently work with their phonogram pal today
To make a formation of a palatial pyramid on a bale of hay.
With wild recognition, we watch these influential acrobats;
Their cautious performance, and completion of their super acts.

"si"

The letters **s** and **i** have two sounds when they swing together in
any syllable after the first one.
Their first sound is "sh" as in ses**si**on, pas**si**on and confes**si**on.

PROFES**SI**ONAL CIRCUS SHOW

The mis**si**on of our next professional group at the big top today
Is a succes**si**on of trapeze artists swinging up and away.
They have been commis**si**oned to do a daring trapeze act.
In this ses**si**on, their timing has to be exact.
Their fearless pas**si**on and nerve is something to behold,
For their profes**si**on is a dangerous commis**si**on, I am told.

Their second sound says, "**zh**," as in version, invasion,
Explosion, ambrosia and occasion.

The invasion of clowns returns to the ring today
With plenty of diversions for us along the way.
First Zach brings a television into the ring,
And Zelda has a version of a song to sing.
Her decision to reach a very high note causes an explosion.
The television is in pieces, and Zach expresses confusion.
They both are stunned and think it must be all an illusion.
On this occasion, we have to say,
What an explosive diversion they brought our way!

"ci"

The letters **c** and **i** like to say, "**sh**," when they are together
in any syllable after the first one as in magician,
Precious, social, facial and musician.

The magician enters this spacious ring to perform a special act.
First he pulls a delicious red apple out of his black top hat.
Waving his wand, saying, "Presto," in an official tone,
He changes that delicious red apple into a precious ruby stone.
We appreciate our efficient and gracious magician, and his act
Of changing into a ruby, the apple he pulled from his top hat.

"ough"
Letters **o,u,g** and **h** have six sounds when they perform together.
Their first sound is like the long sound of the letter o
As in thorough and borough, though and dough.

The thoroughbred horse is galloping around the ring today,
And with him is a doughboy to lead the way.
The doughboy has a basket of doughnuts to reward his horse
For jumping over the wooden boards in the obstacle course.
He thoroughly enjoys putting on this act
With his thoroughbred horse, and that's a fact.

The lion tamer is in the cage with Rusty, the lion, today.
Rusty is r**ough** and shows his teeth and growls our way.
With a mighty crack of the whip, the tamer shows he is t**ough**.
Rusty jumps into the hoop, deciding this one trick is just en**ough**.
What a r**ough** and fierce lion we have performing here.
We hope the t**ough** tamer and Rusty will be back next year.

"ough"
Their third sound makes the sound of "**off**" as in cough.

Farmer Ben has his piglet in the ring today.
Piglet squeals and squawks and wants to play.
Into the pig trough goes the food scraps of the day,
And piglet runs to the feeding trough without delay.
While eating the scraps of food in the trough,
Piglet eats so fast he starts to cough.
Don't gobble your food like this little pig at the trough,
Or you will surely start to cough.

"ough"
The fourth sound is like the **"aw"** sound in law
in words such as th**ough**t and b**ough**t.

This th**ough**tful clown br**ough**t to the big top show
Lots of candy for all of you to take before you go.
We s**ough**t for the best circus acts and put them to rhyme
To make this the most memorable circus of all time.
The clown will be standing at the wr**ough**t iron gate.
So pick up your treat as you leave, but wait!
We have two more acts before you head for the gate.

"ough"
Their fifth sound makes the sound of **"ow"** as in cow
In words such as drought, bough and plough.

Here comes Freddy, the farmer, with his horse and plough.
Attached to his plough is a sturdy leafy tree bough.
Wanting some shade while ploughing his field during the drought,
His use of a tree bough was a cool and clever idea, no doubt.

"ough"
Their sixth sound makes the sound of "**oo**"
As in moon in the word through.

Throughout the years, there have been circus acts,
But never like these ones, and those are the facts.
Our last act is performed by "ough,"
Who is jumping through a flaming hoop just for you
To deliver the news,

NEWS
AN AMAZING
CIRCUS OF
PHONOGRAMS IS
FINALLY THROUGH!
THE END!

"An Amazing Circus of Phonograms is finally through!"
The end!

Mary Jo Nyssen, who has loved reading and writing from an early age, used multisensory phonics to help children learn to spell and read. Nyssen eventually expanded this concept to children's books. Her first, *A Colorful Journey Through the Land of Talking Letters*, won the first-place Purple Dragonfly Book Award for best illustrations and was a Beverly Hills Book Award finalist. Her second, *An Amazing Circus of Phonograms, Act 1*, won the first-place Purple Dragonfly Book Award for picture book ages six and up and was an INDIEFAB finalist for picture books – early readers. She lives with her family in Salem, Oregon.

Joe Palmisano is a professional illustrator. He was born in Brooklyn, New York, and grew up in southern New Jersey. Palmisano lives with his wife and four children in Pennsylvania. His family is the main inspiration for his work. Palmisano has recently decided to write and illustrate his own series of children's books.

Made in the USA
Columbia, SC
13 November 2017